The World of Animals

Joshua BishopRoby

Life Science Readers:
The World of Animals

Publishing Credits

Editorial Director
Dona Herweck Rice

Associate Editor
Joshua BishopRoby

Editor-in-Chief
Sharon Coan, M.S.Ed.

Creative Director
Lee Aucoin

Illustration Manager
Timothy J. Bradley

Publisher
Rachelle Cracchiolo, M.S.Ed.

Science Contributor
Sally Ride Science™

Science Consultants
Thomas R. Ciccone, B.S., M.A. Ed.,
    Chino Hills High School
Dr. Ronald Edwards,
    DePaul University

Teacher Created Materials
5301 Oceanus Drive
Huntington Beach, CA 92649
http://www.tcmpub.com
ISBN 978-0-7439-0593-0
© 2008 Teacher Created Materials, Inc.
Reprinted 2012

Table of Contents

The World of Animals

What do you think of when you hear the word *animal*? You probably think of cats and dogs, or maybe cows or deer. Maybe you think of lizards or whales or even frogs. Do you think of bugs? What about fish? Does the word *animal* make you think of lobsters, sea slugs, or earthworms? These are all members of the animal kingdom.

Some animals we see every day. If you look out the window, can you see birds in the sky? Perhaps you have a pet dog or cat at home. If you went outside and turned over a rock, you could probably find some bugs hiding underneath.

There are many more animals in the world than you might see on a regular day. Some of them are very strange. There are fish that can flop from one pond to another. There are octopuses that can open jars with their tentacles. There is the platypus, which has fur like a cat, a bill like a duck, and a tail like a beaver. It swims in rivers and lays eggs.

There's one animal, though, that you see every day. It is the human being! You are a member of the animal kingdom, too. You are very different from fish, octopuses, and platypuses. There are a lot of things that you have in common, too.

All of these organisms are members of the animal kingdom.

The Language of Taxonomy

A zoologist examines a giant squid.

Jane Goodall is a famous zoologist.

Scientists who study animals are called **zoologists** (ZOO-all-oh-jists). Zoologists need to know exactly which animal other zoologists are talking about. They need to show how animals are alike and different. They use a system called **taxonomy** (TAX-on-oh-mee).

Taxonomy is a system of **classification**. To classify things means to organize them into groups.

Imagine you worked at a car lot. You have many different cars. You have red cars, blue cars, and white cars. You have trucks, sedans, and convertibles. You have cars that run on gas and cars that use electricity. How could you organize them?

You might start by dividing the lot into cars and trucks. Then you might put the cars into two groups. You could have four-door cars and two-door cars. You could split two-door cars into hardtops and convertibles. You could then refer to the different convertibles by their models. There are Continentals, Ramblers, and Boxters. You could say, "The red Boxter needs its tire fixed." If it started raining, you could say, "Get the convertibles inside!"

Zoologists use taxonomy in the same way. A zoologist can talk about an animal by using its scientific name. She might say, "*Felis silvestris* (FEE-lis SIL-ves-tris) make good pets." Other zoologists know she is talking about house cats. Or she can talk about a whole group of animals and use the group's scientific name. She can say, "*Felidae* (FEL-i-day) eat meat." Other scientists know she is talking about all kinds of cats, such as tigers, panthers, and house cats, too.

▼ All of these animals are part of the group that zoologists call *Felidae*.

Carolus Linnaeus

One of the first scientists to use taxonomy was Carolus Linnaeus (lin-AY-us). He wrote a book in 1735. The book classified nature into categories. It started with three categories that Linnaeus called **kingdoms**. One category was for animals. Another was for plants. The third was for rocks and crystals. Each kingdom was split into more categories, just like the car lot.

Since Linnaeus, zoologists have changed taxonomy as they learn new things. They have added new categories. They have switched categories around. They took out the kingdom of rocks. They added kingdoms for fungi, algae, and bacteria. Scientists are still changing taxonomy. It is a work in progress.

Taxonomy now has six kingdoms. *Animalia* (an-uh-MAY-lee-uh) is for animals. It is just one of the kingdoms. Plants, fungi, and microorganisms have their own kingdoms. This book is only about the animal kingdom.

All animals have three things in common. First, living things are made of **cells**, and animals are made of more than one cell. Second, animal cells do not have cell walls like plant cells do. Third, all animals eat other organisms.

This is the taxonomy for a particular type of tarantula, shown below.

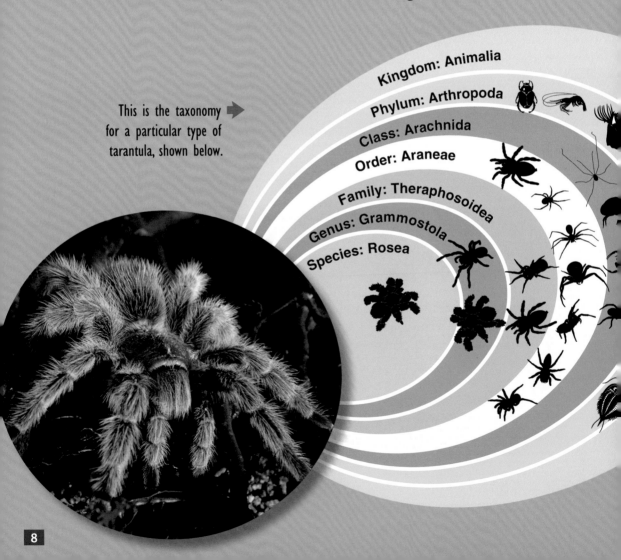

Kingdom: Animalia
Phylum: Arthropoda
Class: Arachnida
Order: Araneae
Family: Theraphosoidea
Genus: Grammostola
Species: Rosea

Kingdoms are divided into groups called **phyla** (FYE-luh). *Animalia* has 17 different phyla. For example, there is a phylum for bugs. There are nine phyla for different kinds of worms! The phylum you know best is *Chordata* (kor-DAY-tuh). Cats, dogs, lizards, and birds are all **chordates**. You are a chordate, too!

Taxonomy keeps dividing. It spreads out like a tree. Each phylum divides into smaller categories called **classes**. For example, all birds are in the *Aves* (AY-veez) class. Classes are split into **orders**. Gorillas and monkeys are in the order Primates. So are humans! Orders have **families**. The next category is **genus**. Then comes **species**.

Every living thing goes into a category at each level. You fall into *Animalia*, *Chordata*, *Mammalia*, *Primates*, *Hominidae* (hah-MIN-uh-day), *Homo*, and *sapiens*. In other words, you are a human being!

Fun Fact

Can you remember "Kids Playing Chicken on Freeways Get Smashed?" If you can, you can remember Kingdom Phylum Class Order Family Genus Species!

Worms, Worms, Worms!

There are thousands of kinds of worms in the world. They wriggle, creep, and crawl. Worms are grouped into nine different phyla. The worms that you know best are *annelids* (AN-el-ids). They are **segmented** worms.

The Nine Phyla of Worms

Annelids—segmented worms

Nematoda—round worms

Platyhelminthes—flat worms

Hemichordata—sea worms

Sipuncula—peanut worms

Nemertea—ribbon worms

Entoprocta—goblet worms

Phoronida—horseshoe worms

Chaetognatha—arrow worms

Worms are simple animals. They have long, tube-shaped bodies. Most have a mouth on one end and an **anus** on the other. They don't even have brains! All they do is eat. They feed off single-celled organisms and waste from other animals.

Some worms in the ocean pull water through their bodies. It goes in through the mouth and out through the anus. Earthworms do the same thing with soil. They burrow through the ground and swallow soil as they go. They digest whatever they can in the soil. What's left passes out the anus.

Earthworms are important to farmers. They churn up the soil as they burrow and ea This makes the soil better for growing crops.

Earth Worm

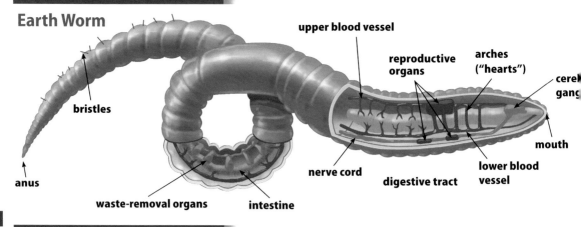

upper blood vessel

reproductive organs

arches ("hearts")

cere gang

bristles

mouth

anus

nerve cord

lower blood vessel

waste-removal organs

intestine

digestive tract

What Are Echinoderms?

Echinoderms (EK-i-no-durms) are animals that live in the ocean. The phylum includes sea urchins, sea stars, and sand dollars. The word is Greek for *spiny skin*. That is what most echinoderms have.

Animals have either bilateral or radial **symmetry**. Bilateral symmetry means that one side of the animal is the mirror image of the other side. Your right hand is a mirror image of your left hand. You have bilateral symmetry.

Radial symmetry means the animal has many identical parts. They are laid out like the spokes on a wheel. All five arms of a sea star are mirror images of one another. It has radial symmetry. In fact, all echinoderms have five-sided radial symmetry.

▲ radial symmetry

◀ bilateral symmetry

Symmetry Isn't Perfect

An animal may have symmetry, but that doesn't mean the sides are perfect copies. The right half of your face has the same parts as the left half. It has eyes, cheekbones, nostrils, ears, and teeth. However, one eye might be just a bit bigger than the other. One ear might be a little higher than the other. The symmetry is only rough. It is not perfect.

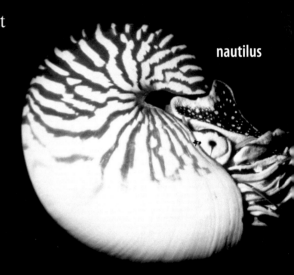

nautilus

Have you ever looked at a snail? Have you seen an octopus? One is slimy and slow. The other is wet and quick. They may look different. But they're both mollusks. The mollusk phylum has many different animals in it. It includes clams, oysters, squid, and octopuses.

Most mollusks have a hard shell, but some don't. Most have a beak-like **radula** (rad-YOU-lah) they use to eat. Clams don't. Many have one "foot" for movement. Squid and octopuses have more than just one. So, why are mollusks all grouped together? Mollusks don't look alike today. But they did millions of years ago.

Zoologists used to group animals together because they looked alike. That makes a **morphological** (MORF-oh-loj-ih-kul) group. It is easy to group animals in this way. It isn't always useful though. Ostriches and humans both have two legs. That doesn't mean they have other things in common, though.

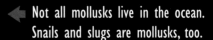
Not all mollusks live in the ocean. Snails and slugs are mollusks, too.

It is more useful to look at animals' **ancestors** (AN-ses-ters). Ancestors are the animals whose offspring became the animal of today. For instance, ostriches and crocodiles are **descended** from dinosaurs. Birds and crocodiles have more in common than ostriches and humans do.

Grouping by ancestors makes **clades** (KLAYDS). Mollusks are a clade. Zoologists studied the cells of living mollusks. They studied the ways that their organs work. They found that slugs are like snails, except without a shell. The tentacles of octopuses work like the feet of oysters. The evidence says that all mollusks share a common ancestor. They should be grouped together.

Cephalopods Have Head Smarts

Mollusks have come a long way. For example, the octopus is thought to be the smartest animal without a spine. Scientists have seen octopuses get through a maze and solve problems. Some octopuses in zoos have learned to open jars of food.

lobster

honeybee

centipede

⬆ Arthropods can be found in the sea, in the air, and on land.

Spiders, flies, centipedes, and scorpions might all be called bugs. Zoologists call them **arthropods** (AR-throw-pawds). Arthropod means "joined foot." All arthropods have legs that move like knights in armor. This is because they have an **exoskeleton** (EX-oh-skel-uh-ton). Your skeleton is inside your body. Theirs is on the outside. It keeps them safe. But they can only move where the exoskeleton is jointed.

There are also other animals with jointed legs. They include lobsters, shrimp, and crabs from the ocean. In fact, these animals share a common ancestor with bugs. You can see the family resemblance if you compare their pictures.

All arthropods have many jointed limbs. Some limbs are used as legs and others for flippers. Still others are used to put food in the animal's mouth. Some centipedes use them to poison their prey! The limbs always come in twos. That is because arthropods have bilateral symmetry. One side is the mirror image of the other side.

Arthropods share another trait. It is **segmentation**. Their bodies are divided into segments. The segments are linked together like cars in a train. The segments can be very similar or very different. Most of a millipede's segments have two legs. A crayfish has segments for walking, for swimming, and for sensing the world around it.

barnacle

Fun Fact!

Have you ever eaten soft-shell crabs? This crab's shell has softened so that it can shed its exoskeleton when it grows larger. The chef cooks these soft-shell crabs, so you can eat the whole crab without worrying about the shell!

What Are Barnacles?

Even though they may not look like it, barnacles are animals, too. In fact, they're arthropods. What might look like a shell is really the barnacle's exoskeleton. What you might think are leaves or tentacles are jointed limbs. Inside the exoskeleton is a segmented animal. It uses its limbs to sweep food into its mouth.

You Are a Chordate

The last major phylum is one you know. Reach around to the middle of your back. Can you feel your **vertebrae** (VER-teh-bray)? Vertebrae are the bones in your backbone. Inside your backbone is your spinal cord. It is a set of nerves that takes messages from your brain to the rest of your body. Your backbone and spinal cord make you a chordate. You are a member of the phylum *Chordata*.

All chordates have or had a notochord. A **notochord** is a stiff structure inside an animal. For most chordates, the notochord is replaced by a stronger backbone. A few chordates never replace the notocord. Others lose it entirely!

Backbones are very useful things to have. Other bones can branch off the backbone to support complex bodies. Muscles can attach to the backbone to move the whole skeleton. The backbone protects the spinal cord. It allows an animal to have a brain that controls the rest of the body. Animals with backbones are called **vertebrates**. Animals without backbones are called **invertebrates**.

Chordata is a phylum, so it is split into classes. There are many classes for fish. Other classes include *Aves* for birds and *Sauropsida* (SAR-op-see-dah) for reptiles. The class *Mammalia* is for mammals. It includes such animals as cats, mice, dogs, and you.

Both humans and snakes have backbones that support the rest of their skeletons.

The stegosaurus' bony plates grow off its backbone.

tunicates

Invertebrate Chordates

There are two kinds of chordates that are not vertebrates. They are called *tunicates* and *lancelets*. Tunicates look a lot like seaweed or coral. Lancelets are tiny ocean creatures. Neither animal ever develops a backbone. Tunicate larvae have notochords, but they lose them when they become adults. Lancelets keep their notochords all their lives.

The World of Fish

There are five classes of fish. The classes are morphological. They are classified by how they look. All fish have gills and live in the water. There are many different kinds of fish. Some have not changed over the years. Zoologists call these **primitive** species. That is because they are a lot like their ancestors.

Hagfish and lampreys are primitive classes of fish. They do not have jaws. Lampreys do have teeth, though. Both types are parasites. That means they live off other living things. Hagfish enter other fish through the mouth, gills, or anus. Then they eat the fish from the inside out. Lampreys attach themselves to other fish and suck their blood.

When you think of fish, you probably think of the animals in the class *Actinopterygii* (ak-ten-op-teh-REEG-ee-eye). They have teeth, jaws, and skeletons made of bone. Jaws allow them to eat different foods, including plants. Some of these fish eat other animals, too. Goldfish and salmon belong in this class.

When it comes to fish with teeth, *Chondrichthyes* (kon-DRICK-tees) reigns supreme. This class includes rays, skates, and sharks. They have teeth and jaws. But their skeletons are made of **cartilage** (CART-ih-lej). You have cartilage in your body. Your nose and ears are made of it.

salmon

The last class of fish may be the weirdest. *Sarcopterygii* (sar-kop-tuh-REEG-ee-eye) fish include *coelacanths* (see-la-KANTH) and lungfish. Other fish only breathe water. Lungfish can breathe air. They live in the mud when summers dry up their streams.

A Long Time in the Dentist's Chair

Sharks have multiple rows of teeth. They lose these teeth constantly and grow new ones to replace them. Over the course of its life, a shark can lose 30,000 teeth!

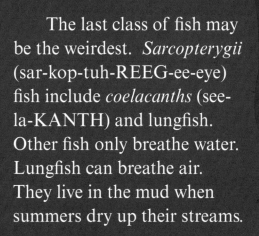

lungfish

Back from the Dead?

Zoologists used to think coelacanths were **extinct**. They could not find any still alive. They only had fossils. Then they found some of these fish deep underwater in the Indian Ocean. These fish are huge. They can grow up to two meters long and weigh 80 kilograms. They are related to the much smaller lungfish.

The Two Lives of Amphibians

salamander

caecilian

You probably know about amphibians (am-FIB-ee-ans) already. Amphibians live in water and on land. That's what *amphibian* means: "two lives." For instance, most frogs are born as tadpoles with no legs. They swim in the water and eat algae. As they grow, they develop legs. They lose their tails. Their gills turn into lungs. Then they live on land as frogs.

The animals that most people think of as amphibians are frogs and toads. They make up almost 90 percent of the amphibian phylum. The other 10 percent are their relatives.

The class is split into three orders. The first order includes frogs and toads. Salamanders make up the second order. They look like lizards, fish, or snakes, but have no scales. A third order is for *caecilians* (suh-SILL-ee-an). They have no legs and are scaled.

Like mollusks, you may wonder why these animals are grouped together. Amphibians are a clade. They all share a common ancestor. Over time, they have changed.

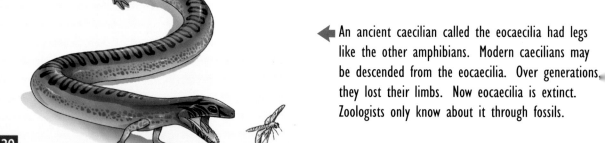

An ancient caecilian called the eocaecilia had legs like the other amphibians. Modern caecilians may be descended from the eocaecilia. Over generations, they lost their limbs. Now eocaecilia is extinct. Zoologists only know about it through fossils.

common frog

grey tree frog

common toad

eastern American toad

poison dart frog

western green toad

Frog or Toad?

What's the difference between frogs and toads? It's not an easy question to answer.

Most frogs are green with smooth skin. The common frog is green with spots. Even the grey tree frog is green!

Most toads are brown and warty. The common toad is not very attractive at all! The eastern American toad is brown. It blends in well with fallen logs and leaves.

There are many exceptions, though. The poison dart frog is bright red. The western green toad lives up to its name. It is green from head to foot.

In the end, there is no good rule as to which is which. It all depends on what the animal was called when it was first discovered.

Dinosaurs and Today's Reptiles

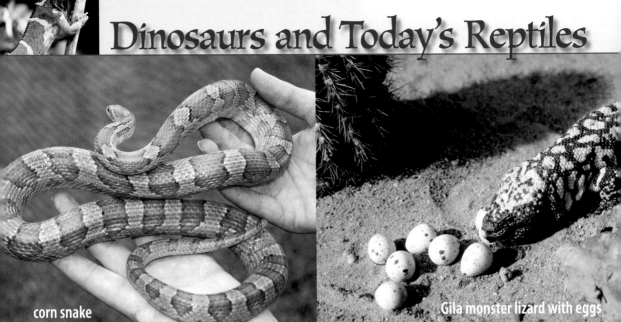

corn snake

Gila monster lizard with eggs

Have you ever watched someone wrestle an alligator? If so, you got a good view of a reptile. Snakes, lizards, turtles, and crocodiles are all reptiles, too. Their class is *Sauropsida*. Reptiles have scales. Most have four legs. But snakes and worm lizards have lost theirs.

Most reptiles lay eggs. Reptile eggs have special **membranes**. This is a thin skinlike layer that protects the egg. Eggs with this special membrane can be bigger than eggs without. Bigger eggs mean bigger animals. Bigger animals lay bigger eggs. Reptiles were the first animals that could get really *huge*!

Dinosaurs were the first large animals on the planet. They were reptiles. Today, the dinosaurs are gone, but other reptiles are still around.

Reptiles can be found on every continent except Antarctica. It is too cold for reptiles there. Reptiles are **ectotherms** (EK-to-therms). Their bodies do not heat themselves. Instead, they

sea turtle

crocodile

lie in the sun to warm up and sit in the shade to cool down. Some reptiles have hearts that can pump backwards. That lets them move warm blood to cold parts of their bodies. Other reptiles can spread out folds of skin to soak in the sun. There are almost as many ways to control body heat as there are reptiles.

All reptiles are descended from a common ancestor. However, reptiles are not a clade. To be a clade, the group would need to include all animals that come from that ancestor. Reptiles are missing some of their relatives: the birds.

frilled lizard ➡

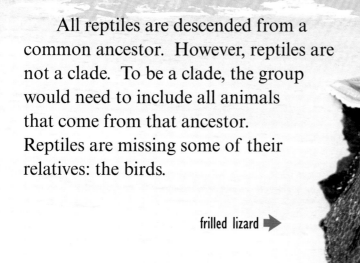

Built for Flight: Birds

owl

ostrich

Birds are some of the most studied animals on the planet. One reason is because they are very common. You will probably see some birds today. Another reason that zoologists study them is because they are fascinating. Birds can do what many wish they could. They can fly.

Birds are built for flight. Almost every part of their bodies helps them fly. Their skeletons are made of hollow bones. This means they have less mass to get into the air. They are **endotherms** (END-oh-therms). That means their bodies keep them warm. They have a lot of energy.

Birds' lungs work twice as hard as yours do. They get oxygen when they inhale and exhale. They never run out of breath. Instead of a stomach, they have a crop and gizzard. In this way, they digest food faster. They need plenty of fuel to beat their wings.

Of course, wings are the birds' greatest feature. Wings are limbs like arms or legs. Feathers cover the wings. Feathers are made of long strings of a material called **protein**. The same kinds of protein are used by other animals to grow hair, scales, nails, and claws.

Not all birds fly, though. Ostriches, penguins, and kiwi are all flightless. Long ago, their ancestors lost the ability to fly. It was too much work! Instead, penguins "fly" through the water to catch fish. Ostriches use their supercharged body to run faster than predators run.

← pigeon skeleton

Last Stop: Mammals

The last class of *Chordata* is *Mammalia* (MAM-al-yah). Mammals feed milk to their young. They also have hair or fur. Nearly all mammals bear live young. Like birds, they are endotherms. Cats, dogs, cows, horses, deer, bears, dolphins, and whales are all mammals. You are a mammal, too.

Mammals are some of the most complex organisms on the planet. They have backbones that let them have complex, sturdy bodies. They have brains that give them habits and instincts to stay alive. They can solve problems and adapt to their surroundings. As endotherms, they have a lot of energy. Combine that with their fur, and they are able to live in very cold places.

As complex as they are, that does not mean that they are the best at everything. Because they breathe air, they can't live on the ocean floor like echinoderms. They have to eat a lot to keep their warm bodies running. Arthropods and amphibians can

◀ Elephants, dogs, cats, gorillas, and whales are all mammals. So are you!

survive on much less. Since they are complex, there are more things that can go wrong. Mammals have more diseases than the rest of the animal kingdom.

There are over 40 different orders of mammals. Cats big and small are in *Carnivora* (KAR-nih-vor-ah). So are wolves, bears, and seals. The biggest order is *Rodentia* (ROW-dent-ya). It has over 2,000 species that include mice, rats, squirrels, and chipmunks. Whales and dolphins are from *Cetecea* (SET-ay-sha). *Primates* (prah-MAY-teez) include monkeys, apes, and humans.

As a human, you can look at the rest of the world of animals and see how you compare. Since you're an endotherm, you don't have to lie out in the sun to warm up like lizards. You have four limbs like amphibians, reptiles, and birds. You have bilateral symmetry. Your left side is a mirror image of your right side. You even have something in common with worms. You use a long tube through your whole body for eating. That tube is your throat, stomach, and intestines.

The world of animals is large and diverse. You're lucky to be a member!

platypus

Monotremes

The echidna and the platypus are from the order *Monotrema*. They are the only mammals to lay eggs. When it was first discovered, a scientist sent a stuffed platypus to Europe. Everyone thought it was a fake! They tried to find the stitches that connected the "otter" with the "duck's bill."

Whale Pattern Baldness

Like other mammals, whales have hair. They are born with a little fuzz on their skin. As they grow up, they lose the fuzz. For the rest of their lives, they have no hair. But they did when they were born!

Whose mouth is cleaner? You can test the saliva from a dog and from a human to see which grows more bacteria fastest. In addition to the materials, you'll need a friendly dog for this lab! Be sure to wash your hands between each step, and carefully clean or discard your materials afterwards.

Materials

- eight sterile nutrient agar Petri dishes (can be ordered online)

- marker and labels

- cotton swabs

- pencil and chart for recording observations

- camera for taking photos (especially digital or Polaroid)

Procedure

1 Check to be sure your Petri dishes are clean. Place a label on the lid of each dish. Mark the labels with the date. Number each, 1–8. Label dishes 1–4 DOG. Label dishes 5–8 HUMAN.

2 Before eating breakfast, collect saliva samples from your dog and your own mouth. Use a sterile cotton swab to collect saliva from the inside of the dog's mouth. Make sure the saliva is not taken from outside the dog's mouth. Once outside, it could pick up bacteria from the dog's coat, your carpet, or other places.

3 Open dish 1 DOG. Gently wipe the saliva-coated swab across the agar. Close the dish with its labeled lid. Set it in a safe place, at room temperature. Take a picture of the dish.

4 Use a new cotton swab. Collect saliva from your own mouth. Deposit the sample in dish 5 HUMAN. Follow the procedures above.

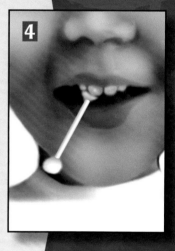

5 Chart your activities.

6 Repeat the procedures for gathering saliva samples during the evening hours, the next morning, and the next evening. Use new dishes each time and chart your activities.

7 Beginning a day after each sample is collected, chart changes observed in each dish. Rate the bacteria growth in each: none, a little, or a lot. Take pictures each day.

8 After five days of recordings for each sample, draw conclusions. Label the pictures with the dish number, as well as the time and date of the photograph.

9 Summarize your findings.

Glossary

ancestor—a primitive animal species that developed into modern species

Animalia—the animal kingdom; animals are multicellular, have no cell walls, and eat other organisms

anus—the opening through which an animal discards waste

arthropod—an animal with an exoskeleton and jointed limbs

cartilage—a material softer than bone used in animal skeletons

cells—the building blocks of life

chordate—animals that have a notochord at one point in their life

clade—a group of animals descended from a common ancestor

class—the third level of taxonomy, between phylum and order

classification—a system by which things are categorized

descended—came from

echinoderm—a marine animal with five-sided radial symmetry; sea stars and sand dollars

ectotherm—an animal that relies on its surroundings to maintain its heat

endotherm—an animal that can produce its own heat

exoskeleton—a hard body structure on the outside of an animal

extinct—when there are no living members of a species

family—the fifth level of taxonomy, between order and genus

genus—the sixth level of taxonomy, between family and species

invertebrate—an animal without a backbone

kingdom—the first level of taxonomy, divided into phyla

membrane—a skinlike layer that separates living tissues

morphological—organized by shape

notochord—stiff structure inside an animal that allows more complex organization

order—the fourth level of taxonomy, between class and family

phylum (phyla)—the taxonomy level between kingdom and class

primitive—an animal that has not changed much from its ancestor

protein—a tough material animals use to grow body features

radula—a beaklike organ that many mollusks use to eat

segmented—separated into different parts of the whole

species—the lowest level of taxonomy; a specific kind of animal

symmetry—the way an organism is structured; can be bilateral (two sides) or radial (spokes on a wheel)

taxonomy—a system of names

vertebrae—the bones that make up your backbone

vertebrate—an animal with a backbone

zoologist—an animal scientist

Index

Sally Ride
Science

Sally Ride Science

Sally Ride Science™ is an innovative content company dedicated to fueling young people's interests in science. Our publications and programs provide opportunities for students and teachers to explore the captivating world of science—from astrobiology to zoology. We bring science to life and show young people that science is creative, collaborative, fascinating, and fun.